I'm Off to College, Now WHAT?

Survival Tips for this New Journey

Cindy Laubenstein

ISBN: 978-0-692-91080-1 (sc)
ISBN: 978-1-4834-8242-2 (e)

For more information go to:
www.aspirecollege consulting.org

Illustrations Created by:

StickFigure People
https://stickfigurepeople.selz.com

Book Layout Design by: Donna Savas

Lulu Publishing Services rev. date: 03/22/2018

Dedicated to all the students with whom I have worked, especially those who struggled to get there and to all students who work so hard to prepare themselves to make a positive contribution to our future.

With love and respect to my two very own college students, Lindsey and Kyle. I am so proud of you!

CONTENTS

CONGRATULATIONS!

YOU'RE GOING TO COLLEGE!

You have made a big decision on where you plan to spend the next four years (at least) of your life. The first step that will set you on a path for the journey of a lifetime. Amidst the chaos that is high school prep, college search, campus visits, major considerations, essays, recommendation letters, research and speculation, you've finally made it! You've been accepted, you've made your choice, and you're on your way!

Many emotions come with the transition; likely excitement filled with some trepidation and maybe even a little anxiety. You may have heard it said by now that the next four years are likely to be looked back upon as some of the best times of your life. While you will probably never have another experience quite like it, your freshman year is likely to be filled with many ups and downs as you broaden your horizons and encounter an abundance of new people and experiences.

This book is designed to provide some tips to ease the transition into college life; to offer some ideas that will help to propel you towards success and help you navigate any bumps in the road should they rise up to meet you. Stay humble during the good times, and recognize through any challenging moments that they are most likely only temporary.

Put together a plan to overcome obstacles along the way and applaud your victories, no matter how big or small!

Before you begin, take the time to say
"Thank You" to those who helped you get here.

The key to real happiness in life is gratitude.
Continue to show gratitude by working hard and excelling at
academic and personal excellence throughout this journey.

Remember to stay focused on your ultimate goal:
To graduate with a 'ticket' that will open
doors for the rest of your life.

Enjoy each section of this book as they focus on
excellence in three areas:

Academic   Social   Personal

As you read, you may want to make note of some personal goals to set for yourself. At the back of the book, make use of the semester schedules to help with time management and record special moments along the way.

ACADEMIC SUCCESS

GO TO CLASS

S oon after courses begin, you may notice some students from your dorm or classes beginning to skip class, opting to sleep in. Avoid falling into this habit as it can be costly in the end. Know that as many as one in three freshman don't return for sophomore year for a host of reasons; one being academic struggles due to lack of focus on studies.

While skipping class can easily become a habit, you may be short-changing yourself. The professor is apt to place emphasis on areas of importance from the text (if they choose to use a text) that may be an indication of material that may show up again on the exam. Sleeping in could cost valuable time in the long run should you miss important lectures.

Understand the instructor's attendance policy. This can save you from the shock of receiving a poor grade at the end of the semester. Also, understand attendance requirements as they relate to any financial aid received.

GPA will be important if you are trying to maintain any scholarship monies and it is likely to matter as you approach the end of this journey and you're in the hunt for your first job. Just like in high school, freshman year is a good time to try to create a 'cushion' for yourself to compensate for any possible slip-ups along the way.

SIT NEAR THE FRONT

Although you may at some point end up with an eight o'clock class (it's bound to happen!), there is still a benefit to sitting near the front where you are not likely to maintain focus. Studies indicate a high correlation between your grade in the class and where you sit in the classroom. Not only are you more likely to engage in the classroom through listening and participation, but the professor may make a mental note that you wanted to succeed in that class. And they may even recognize you when you drop by the office later.

Speak up in class and ask questions about the material. The teacher will be flattered that you cared enough to support their efforts to engage fellow students.

DEVELOP RELATIONSHIPS WITH PROFESSORS

One of the biggest mistakes college students make is never forming a relationship with their professors. Engagement with professors can enhance your college experience in so many ways! Professors can serve as sounding boards on issues such as classes, majors, etc. and often times will schedule special sessions and activities where students can become involved both academically as well as socially.

Stop by and meet the professor during their stated office hours. It is best to go with a purpose in mind; i.e., to ask for clarification about course material, bounce around an idea, or get help with an area that you don't quite understand. You may very well get a better grade if your professor knows that you took the time to visit and show an interest in succeeding in the class. It can make a difference with a potential borderline grade! If you feel that you learned a lot from the course, let the professor know. He will appreciate it and may even remember you.

In addition, professors can be a wonderful contact as they can:

1. Serve as a reference for an internship, co-op or employment opportunity.
2. Give you a lead on where to begin to find on-campus part-time jobs, summer opportunities, etc.
3. Be a member of a faculty committee that determines recipients for internal college and departmental scholarships.
4. Invite you to assist with a research project.
5. Ask you to become a Teacher's Assistant.

SEEK OUT A MENTOR

L ook for a mentor along this journey! Start early. A mentor can be a professor, a teaching assistant or administrator who takes a special liking to you or with whom you form a deeper bond. Your network of professors and contacts will likely lead to relationships that will benefit you in many ways. A mentor can be a strong supporter throughout your college life and may also be your lead on a potential internships or job as you approach graduation.

GET ORGANIZED

Getting and staying organized will save so much stress that comes with missing assignments, forgetting meetings, running late and feeling overwhelmed.

Keep a to-do list stored in your cell phone or in an agenda, planner or small notebook. Make a note of deadlines. Consider setting an alert that will notify you of upcoming deadlines ahead.

Make a habit of being ten minutes early whenever possible. Arriving early can help de-stress and allows more time to chat and begin to build relationships with fellow students or even the professor.

FIND YOUR CLASSES BEFORE THE FIRST DAY

This is a great way to make a new friend! Seek out a new dorm mate and see if they have time to stroll around campus and find classroom locations. It could alleviate stress and save a lot of time the first week of classes if you know where you are going and how to get there.

Put the transportation app on your phone (almost all schools have them now) so you can keep up with bus schedules and locations. You may want to do a practice run.

ESTABLISH AND MANAGE YOUR SCHEDULE

A typical college freshman schedule may look something like this:

	Monday	Tuesday	Wednesday	Thursday	Friday
8am					
9	GBUS160		GBUS160		GBUS160
10	GECON200	GPSYCH101	GECON200	GPSYCH101	GECON200
11					
12pm	MATH205		MATH205		MATH205
1		GCOMH 123		GCOMH 123	
2					
3	MKT101				
4					
5				SPK100	

Add in other commitments and extra-curricular activities like study sessions, clubs, sports, exercise, Greek life, etc. and it can fill up quickly.

It will be necessary to develop a study schedule different from your high school schedule of generally studying in the evening after practices, rehearsals and dinner are completed. Take advantage of pockets of time throughout your daily schedule and you may find more time for extracurricular activities and, most importantly ... sleep!

TREAT ACADEMICS LIKE A JOB

SCHEDULE A 35 HOUR 'WORK' WEEK FOR STUDYING.

O nce you've laid out your classes on your calendar, plan blocks of time to study throughout the week. Try to take advantage of open slots for studying and completing assignments. Schedule a 35 hour 'work week' for studying. With advance planning, you may find that it is possible to fit in all the academic responsibilities and social activities and still have time for yourself. Before each week, be realistic about how much time you can devote to social activities and how much time you're going to need to spend reading, writing or crunching numbers based on test schedules and academic expectations.

Check out the blank schedules at the end of this book to help you get you started.

ESTABLISH GOOD STUDY HABITS

D etermine what study environment works best for you. Some people feel motivated being around others in a study group or the library; some prefer total silence while others enjoy music or even television in the background. Find out what habits and environment work best for you and where you are best able to maximize the time you have. Learn if you are a morning person or a night owl; when you are most productive. The sooner you figure this out, the more easily you can adapt to your schedule.

Give yourself incentives to study. Don't cash your paycheck or buy the t-shirt until you're finished with your project or assignment. Celebrate with friends after you've studied for and taken the test. Treat yourself to something you've been wanting after you reach your studying goals; a dessert, a new sweatshirt, or a Frisbee game on the quad with friends.

DON'T GET BEHIND!

A s a matter of fact, stay one step ahead! No one ever said "Darn, I started on that assignment too early!"

Time management is key and one of the toughest things to do in college. It will seem as though you have a lot of free time, therefore plenty of time to get work completed.

It is easy to procrastinate. It's better to do things as soon as possible, especially your homework. Make it a point to schedule time throughout your schedule to work on homework and complete class assignments early before engaging in any other recreations.

GET HELP

E very college has a multitude of resources to help you, however most colleges expect you to self-identify; i.e., it is up to YOU to ASK for help when you need it. If you feel that you are struggling, seek out help through office visits, study sessions and tutors. There is nothing wrong with asking for help. Don't wait until it is too late!

Simply tell your professor, "I'm struggling with this class, but I want to succeed. What do you recommend?" Most professors are happy to know that a student is interested and genuinely wants to succeed, and they will generally be glad to give assistance.

School librarians can also be a great source of help on research projects; use them, just ask!

REGISTER AS EARLY AS POSSIBLE!

M ake this a habit. It will pay off in better schedules and can help avoid early morning and late evening classes as well as being forced to delay classes critical to your area of study. You may even be able to target certain preferred professors. But keep in mind that your opinion of a teacher could be quite different from that of another student.

Go to the office to request an instructor for advice on how to get added to a full or over-enrolled course. Do not send a pleading email. Drop by the office, introduce yourself and ask if he or she has time to talk. State that you would like to add the course and why. If you cannot track down the professor, send an email stating that you have tried to make the request in person and explain your situation. Remember, when sending email, DO NOT USE ALL CAPS.

Recognize that professors often have no control over who gets open slots as they tend to get filled quickly as students drop a course. It is in your best interest to constantly check registration or set an alert on your phone as spaces are often filled within minutes of becoming available.

Additional tips:

For planning your schedule, consider courseoff.com. To see teacher ratings and history for a particular class or teacher, try ratemyprofessors.com. Explore coursicle.com to be alerted when space opens up n a previously full schedule.

DON'T OVERLOAD YOURSELF FIRST SEMESTER

Take a mix of classes but don't strive to get all of your rigorous classes out of the way in the first semester. College is hard; and if your scholarship hinges on a particular grade point average, you may want to make sure you ease into the challenging courses instead of hitting multiple tough classes head on just as you are getting acclimated to your new environment.

If your university has an honors college and you want to be accepted, learn the GPA requirements and when you are eligible to apply. Keep this in mind when planning your course schedule and your study schedule!

Consider making use of any AP credits to buy yourself a free period or to help get ahead in credit hours.

CONNECT WITH
THE TUTOR LAB

A s you seek out your classroom locations, also take time to find the tutor lab. Get an understanding of how to book a tutor and if there are specific requirements to take advantage of these services. Often times peer tutors are free or come at a very minimal cost.

Recognize that planning ahead can be of utmost importance once classes begin. Schedule time with a peer tutor at the first sign of challenge in a rigorous course. You will be glad you did!

If you know that you are taking a super challenging course, you may want to line up a tutor before hitting a rough spot in the course. In some schools it can take a week or two to reserve a spot so connect with a tutor as soon as possible.

SET ACADEMIC GOALS

Going through college without goals is like running a race with no finish line. Take some time to reflect on all the work you've put in to get you this far and what you hope to get out of this journey through college. Think of goals to set for yourself, both short and long term. Give yourself incentives to reach both short and long term goals.

Maybe you want to strive for a certain GPA that will guarantee that you maintain your scholarship. Or maybe you want to become involved in at least two campus organizations. Complete your project before you buy the sweatshirt. Focus for a two hour window before you go running. Achieve your 35 hour work week before a big weekend. Consider meeting a couple of professors in your chosen field and ask about recommendations to pursue employment in that field. Or just take the opportunity to meet each professor.

Whatever your goals, write them down. It will be much easier to finish the race if you have a finish line!

MY GOALS:

Academic

_____
_____
_____
_____
_____
_____

Social

_____
_____
_____
_____
_____
_____

Personal

_____
_____
_____
_____
_____
_____

CHECK YOUR EMAIL FREQUENTLY

S ome students feel that email is old-fashioned and out of style. It is still the way adults and colleges will communicate with you.

Be aware of each professor's method and site for communicating and assigning work. This may be different from your student portal or class syllabus.

Understand how the college is likely to communicate important things such as new scholarships available, dining hall closings, inclement weather updates, transportation issues, etc. Don't' miss out.

GIVE MUCH THOUGHT TO YOUR CHOICE OF MAJOR

Consider your options based on your interests and your areas of strength. Once you have an idea of which occupation you would like to explore, look at the market for that type of work. Understand the job outlook and educational requirements. The Bureau of Labor and Statistics Occupational Outlook Handbook is a good place to start (www. bls.gov/ooh). This is of utmost importance, especially in times of high unemployment.

Listen to other opinions but do your own research. Remember that you are the one who will have to spend time in this vocation. Talk with and shadow others in the field and seek out opportunities for internships in areas of interest to determine if you are on track to meet your aspirations. Also consider if this is an area where you will be happy to devote the majority of your time.

You could work in this field for 30, 40 even 50 years. It is worth it to do some research up front and explore potential careers in greater detail.

TAKE A BROAD RANGE OF CLASSES

Step outside of your comfort zone and your chosen field of study. It is a good idea to expose yourself to different subjects, fields and themes. Over half of all college students change their major at least once during their undergraduate stay, with many changing their major two or three times before settling on one.

A class or two in other fields can increase your options down the road if, or more likely when, you shift directions to another career. Knowledge and understanding in other areas can be of great benefit. Similar to changes in major, you may very well be in a different field at the end of your career from where you started.

TAKE ADVANTAGE OF OPPORTUNITIES TO IMPROVE YOUR WRITING SKILLS

Almost all colleges and universities offer writing workshops, tutors and other resources to help you develop strong writing skills. The best part is they're usually free! This is a competency that can always be improved regardless of your in-coming level of strength. It is a wonderful resource that will pay big dividends in college and beyond! Make time to attend classes and workshops early in your college journey.

UNDERSTAND THE GRADUATION REQUIREMENTS FOR YOUR MAJOR

Most degree programs require 120 hours to graduate. So, this means that you will need to take 15 hours per semester in order to graduate in four years.

If you register for less than 15 hours, don't expect the college to bring to your attention that you will be short if aiming to complete your degree in four years. You will need to manage your credits to graduate within your intended window.

Should you need to drop a class, determine if your school has a program that will allow you to add on a class within the first week or two to make up for those lost credits. Come up with a plan to make up those hours if you find that you are coming up short. Summer and/or on-line courses could be an option if you come up short.

FAMILIARIZE YOURSELF WITH THE CAREER RESOURCES CENTER

Four years will go by quickly. Remember your ultimate goal is to GET A JOB! Yes, IN ALL CAPS! That's why you're here. Find out how your college can help with internships, co-ops, summer job opportunities and, ultimately, finding a job, or at least point you towards interview opportunities.

Get to know the people and how their services can help you. It may be as simple as helping develop a resume and cover letter. The Career Resources Center is likely to be a wonderful resource to help you in your quest for employment.

Don't wait until senior year! That could be a big mistake. Seek out services early in your college journey so that you are better equipped to carve a path that will lead to ultimate success: a job!

CAREER CENTER

SOCIAL ENGAGEMENT

STEP OUT OF YOUR COMFORT ZONE

O nce on campus, seek out ways to meet others and begin to form relationships. Introduce yourself to other students on your dorm floor with an understanding that you may all experiencing some trepidation at this point.

While you may be invited to a fraternity (or other) party early on, know that there are many other ways to make friends if that is not your style. Engaging with classmates and showing up to learn more about clubs and organizations is a great way to get started.

If you do choose the party atmosphere, always be aware of what is going into your body and understand that alcohol will decrease your inhibitions. Try to establish a 'buddy' who will look out for you and one whose back you will always have as well.

While parties may result in fast friends, remember that developing friends through other similarities can be more meaningful but can take more time. Don't become frustrated early in the game. Take the time to get to know others by engaging in campus activities and joining clubs and organizations. Lasting relationships are well worth the extra time and effort in the long run.

MAINTAIN REALISTIC EXPECTATIONS

I t will take time to establish a network of friends and acquaintances. Don't allow yourself to become discouraged if you feel that you have not made close friends within the first month or two. Reach out to new people in class and have in mind some clubs and activities that you want to explore to begin to build your network once you reach campus. Part-time jobs on campus are another route to forming friendships.

Remember that it takes multiple interactions to develop meaningful relationships. The best way to make friends is through others with whom you have something in common; such as a club, organization, extra-curricular activity, a job or an opportunity within your field of study. Keep in mind that you may only meet once or twice a month so it may take time to bond under these circumstances. Invite potential friends to the gym or to a pick-up game of basketball or even to grab coffee.

GET INVOLVED IN CLUBS AND CAMPUS TRADITIONS

C ollege events differ from the compulsory events you might have done in high school. One big difference is that college students attend because they genuinely want to be involved, not because it will help to build their high school resume and look good for colleges. The real draw is the opportunity to belong to a group with similar interests and goals. The ability to build a bigger network is worth the effort so get involved and expose yourself to new experiences. Also consider opportunities for organizations within your area of study. Maybe an investments club, a service organization or a group that welcomes students who are working towards a degree in education, nursing, or engineering. You get the point. Opportunities abound in college! Take advantage.

Should you find yourself in an environment where you already know a lot of people, probably from your high school, take the time to explore clubs and events outside of your established and comfortable social circle. While it's fine to invite your best friends to participate, this could prevent you from meeting another potential friend. If it interests you, show up! There will be many others like you who are exploring new interests.

FIND A PASSION

Take time to peruse the college website, go to the student center or attend a student organization fair to have an understanding of all the opportunities for involvement. Reflect on what you enjoy doing and what you're genuinely interested in. Seek out opportunities to immerse yourself in campus organizations and activities.

University planned altruistic projects such as Habitat for Humanity or organized fundraisers to support a cause are a great way to give back to a worthy cause throughout your college years and develop new friendships. Colleges as well as specific organizations are likely to adopt a cause; somewhere where you can make a difference in the lives of others in need. Get involved! Consider Cancer Awareness, Big Brothers/ Big Sisters or similar groups. Helping others who may be less fortunate than you is one of the best things that you can do for your mental health and the rewards will far surpass your sacrifice of time and effort.

The relationships you develop will be invaluable throughout your college journey and beyond!

ESTABLISH CLEAR COMMUNICATION WITH YOUR ROOMMATE

Conflicts may arise over music, sleep schedules, food, clothing, messiness, visitors, etc. Establish boundaries early and set clear ground rules.

Clear communication and mutual respect for each other is key. Take this opportunity to communicate your feelings while also listening to your roommate's concerns and work towards an acceptable solution should concerns arise. Lend an understanding ear and be willing to compromise.

Should the situation be unbearable, your Resident Advisor is a valuable resource to help with a compromise or help switch roommates.

SUPPORT ATHLETICS AND THE ARTS

While you are likely to attend college football or basketball games (depending on your school), take the time to attend and support other sports as well. If you know someone who plays lacrosse, field hockey or volleyball, for example, go to a game to support them. They will be grateful that you took the time and you will likely make a forever friend.

It's also very rewarding to show up for performances and support friends in theater, orchestra or an a cappella group. Amazing talent abounds on college campuses.

Take advantage of performing arts center performances as they offer some of the best entertainment at a reasonable cost. Seek out some of these performances, especially when your parents come to visit.

ESTABLISH AS MANY FRIENDSHIPS AS POSSIBLE, BUT CHOOSE YOUR FRIENDS BASED ON YOU!

First, remember that we are all unique. You are truly one of a kind so don't compare yourself to others. There will always be people who appear to be better than and not as good as you in all areas of life. Listen to others, but form your own opinions about teachers, other students, careers, social activities and campus involvement. As you begin to meet people, remember that true friendships develop over time. Be patient but continue to work to develop relationships that are compatible with your interests and values.

Depending on the size of your school, you may find the number of new people a bit intimidating. Everyone feels that way at first. Get beyond the intimidation and you'll find dozens and maybe hundreds of people that you get along with and can learn from. Friendships will provide amazing experiences that will give you great memories as you look back later in life.

WHAT ABOUT ME?

GET REST

A time may likely come in your freshman year where you may feel that you have 'hit a wall' and you're not sure if you can keep on going. Studies, activities, time management and responsibilities may have you burning the candle at both ends thus squeezing in on valuable sleep time. The first thing to do? Get a good night's sleep. Sleep deprivation can alter your brain's way of thinking, thereby altering your perspective on your day to day ability to function. Feeling refreshed can give you the power to develop a plan to get out of your temporary slump.

Did you know? Students who routinely stay up late on weeknights perform worse than students who get lasting sleep on a regular basis. Getting sufficient rest will give you more energy, improve your brain function, boost your immune system, and enhance your emotional well-being. Try to make it a habit.

EAT HEALTHY

The college meal plan can be an invitation to overeat when there is so much food at your disposal at every meal, often overloaded with carb laden choices. Focus on a balanced diet of lean meat or protein, fruits and vegetables and whole grains. Avoid sugar, sodas, saturated fats and high intake of carbs. You will feel better and be in better shape to avoid the infamous "Freshman 15".

Eat breakfast. Fueling your brain before classes will help improve your concentration and your short-term memory. If you can't make it to the dining hall every day, start with a healthy snack to help boost your brain power to start your day. You may want to make other arrangements if your meal plan only allows two meals a day and you use those for lunch and dinner. Consider a protein bar or other energy boost breakfast that can sustain you through the morning hours. More small meals can be healthier that two meals per day.

EXERCISE!

IT'S A MIRACLE DRUG!

E xercise helps us control our weight, combat health conditions and diseases like high cholesterol and heart disease, improves mood and boosts energy. Try to get in 30 minutes of walking at least. Join an intramural sports team, do laps at the pool or sign up for exercise classes at the recreation center.

When you feel that you may have hit that wall, after getting a good nights' sleep, get some exercise. Go for a walk (with a new friend if you can), ride a bike or play Frisbee in the quad. Fresh air and increasing your heart rate can do wonders for your attitude.

Recognize that this may likely be the only time in your life that you have a free gym membership. Use it!

PROTECT YOUR MIND AND BODY

N ow that you are responsible for your own comings and goings, you are the one in charge of YOU. **MAKE WISE DECISIONS!** There will likely be no one else looking out for your best interest around the clock. Take a moment to think about choices before you jump in to risky situations and understand that choices in the moment can have lasting consequences.

Never leave a drink alone. Don't believe it when you hear "Go ahead. It's okay. Everybody does it." (Everybody doesn't do 'it'). Remember it's okay to choose new friends, groups, etc.

You have been given one mind and body. Protect yourself by making wise choices. Try to protect your friends should you be given the opportunity.

BUDGET YOUR EXPENSES

C ollege may be the first opportunity for you to manage your own finances in preparation for being an adult. Part of responsible money management is having a budget and staying within your spending limits. Know your monthly allowance and be cognizant of any large payments that may come up in the next few months or significant purchases you wish to make; i.e., fraternity dues, ski weekend, etc. Attempt to spend less than your monthly allowance to save enough to cover larger expenses in later months. Keep track of where your money is going and change spending habits in order to stay within your monthly allowance or save for an upcoming event.

Assuming tuition, room and board have already been paid for, a sample budget may look like this:

Total amount of allowance per month:	*$100*
Food/groceries:	*$40*
Utilities:	*$25*
Supplies:	*$15*
Discretionary:	*$20*

Seek out scholarships annually to help with your expenses. These are often communicated in the fall for the upcoming year.

VISIT THE UNIVERSITY HEALTH CENTER AND/OR COUNSELING CENTER

The university health center will have all sorts of information about staying healthy on campus, in addition to doctors and staff on hand to handle issues common to college students. Take advantage of the free amenities your health center offers: free vaccines, condoms, birth control and counseling are among the most common.

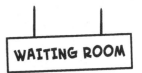

Should feelings of depression or anxiety overwhelm you, make a visit to the counseling center. The staff there is skilled in handling these issues among college students, that's their expertise. Conversations will be confidential and you may have a new perspective to help you get through some rough bumps in the road. And remember, these rough moments are most likely temporary. Put together a plan and find the support to help you succeed.

UTILIZE THE COLLEGE SAFETY DEPARTMENT

A lmost all colleges and universities have a public safety department that looks after the safety of the student population. Know how to contact the safety officers who will routinely:

- Escort you to your home or dorm if you feel unsafe. Keep this in mind if you are leaving the library late at night and feel unsafe walking alone.

- Give you valuable safety tips about living in your area (especially applicable in an urban setting).

- Investigate crimes that happen on campus. If you've been a victim of a crime, especially robbery, rape, coercion, or assault, notify campus security and/or local police.

Report any suspicious activity on campus to the safety department.

BUILDING YOUR NETWORK

W hile you have your college and your intended area of study that will lead to your ultimate major, the real key to success will be the relationships you make along the way.

The people you meet and the relationships that you build can lead to wonderful experiences and opportunities beyond college.

These are the people you may travel with, request a virtual introduction with, network with for job prospects, request a recommendation from and most likely cross paths with again at some point down the road. Take advantage of every opportunity to build your network. And help others along the way every chance you get. It will likely be remembered for a lifetime.

SCHEDULING AND
JOURNAL PAGES

MY FRESHMAN FIRST
SEMESTER SCHEDULE

	MONDAY	TUESDAY	WEDNESDAY
6:00 a.m.			
7:00 a.m.			
8:00 a.m.			
9:00 a.m.			
10:00 a.m.			
11:00 a.m.			
12:00 p.m.			
1:00 p.m.			
2:00 p.m.			
3:00 p.m.			
4:00 p.m.			
5:00 p.m.			
6:00 p.m.			
7:00 p.m.			
8:00 p.m.			
9:00 p.m.			
10:00 p.m.			
11:00 p.m.			
12:00 a.m.			
1:00 a.m.			

MY FRESHMAN FIRST
SEMESTER SCHEDULE

THURSDAY	FRIDAY	SATURDAY	SUNDAY

MY FRESHMAN SECOND SEMESTER SCHEDULE

	MONDAY	TUESDAY	WEDNESDAY
6:00 a.m.			
7:00 a.m.			
8:00 a.m.			
9:00 a.m.			
10:00 a.m.			
11:00 a.m.			
12:00 p.m.			
1:00 p.m.			
2:00 p.m.			
3:00 p.m.			
4:00 p.m.			
5:00 p.m.			
6:00 p.m.			
7:00 p.m.			
8:00 p.m.			
9:00 p.m.			
10:00 p.m.			
11:00 p.m.			
12:00 a.m.			
1:00 a.m.			

MY FRESHMAN SECOND
SEMESTER SCHEDULE

THURSDAY	FRIDAY	SATURDAY	SUNDAY

MEMORIES FROM FRESHMAN YEAR

My roommate(s):

Favorite professor:

Most interesting class:

Memories from the dorm:

Organizations I joined:

Best food in the dining hall:

New friends:

Lessons I learned:

Challenges:

WHAT I WISH I KNEW THEN
THAT I KNOW NOW:

_____
_____
_____
_____
_____
_____
_____
_____
_____

NEW GOALS I NOW HAVE SET:

_____
_____
_____
_____
_____
_____
_____
_____
_____

YEAR TWO FIRST
SEMESTER SCHEDULE

	MONDAY	TUESDAY	WEDNESDAY
6:00 a.m.			
7:00 a.m.			
8:00 a.m.			
9:00 a.m.			
10:00 a.m.			
11:00 a.m.			
12:00 p.m.			
1:00 p.m.			
2:00 p.m.			
3:00 p.m.			
4:00 p.m.			
5:00 p.m.			
6:00 p.m.			
7:00 p.m.			
8:00 p.m.			
9:00 p.m.			
10:00 p.m.			
11:00 p.m.			
12:00 a.m.			
1:00 a.m.			

YEAR TWO FIRST
SEMESTER SCHEDULE

THURSDAY	FRIDAY	SATURDAY	SUNDAY

YEAR TWO SECOND SEMESTER SCHEDULE

	MONDAY	TUESDAY	WEDNESDAY
6:00 a.m.			
7:00 a.m.			
8:00 a.m.			
9:00 a.m.			
10:00 a.m.			
11:00 a.m.			
12:00 p.m.			
1:00 p.m.			
2:00 p.m.			
3:00 p.m.			
4:00 p.m.			
5:00 p.m.			
6:00 p.m.			
7:00 p.m.			
8:00 p.m.			
9:00 p.m.			
10:00 p.m.			
11:00 p.m.			
12:00 a.m.			
1:00 a.m.			

YEAR TWO SECOND SEMESTER SCHEDULE

THURSDAY	FRIDAY	SATURDAY	SUNDAY

YEAR THREE FIRST SEMESTER SCHEDULE

	MONDAY	TUESDAY	WEDNESDAY
6:00 a.m.			
7:00 a.m.			
8:00 a.m.			
9:00 a.m.			
10:00 a.m.			
11:00 a.m.			
12:00 p.m.			
1:00 p.m.			
2:00 p.m.			
3:00 p.m.			
4:00 p.m.			
5:00 p.m.			
6:00 p.m.			
7:00 p.m.			
8:00 p.m.			
9:00 p.m.			
10:00 p.m.			
11:00 p.m.			
12:00 a.m.			
1:00 a.m.			

YEAR THREE FIRST SEMESTER SCHEDULE

THURSDAY	FRIDAY	SATURDAY	SUNDAY

YEAR THREE SECOND SEMESTER SCHEDULE

	MONDAY	TUESDAY	WEDNESDAY
6:00 a.m.			
7:00 a.m.			
8:00 a.m.			
9:00 a.m.			
10:00 a.m.			
11:00 a.m.			
12:00 p.m.			
1:00 p.m.			
2:00 p.m.			
3:00 p.m.			
4:00 p.m.			
5:00 p.m.			
6:00 p.m.			
7:00 p.m.			
8:00 p.m.			
9:00 p.m.			
10:00 p.m.			
11:00 p.m.			
12:00 a.m.			
1:00 a.m.			

YEAR THREE SECOND SEMESTER SCHEDULE

THURSDAY	FRIDAY	SATURDAY	SUNDAY

YEAR FOUR FIRST SEMESTER SCHEDULE

	MONDAY	TUESDAY	WEDNESDAY
6:00 a.m.			
7:00 a.m.			
8:00 a.m.			
9:00 a.m.			
10:00 a.m.			
11:00 a.m.			
12:00 p.m.			
1:00 p.m.			
2:00 p.m.			
3:00 p.m.			
4:00 p.m.			
5:00 p.m.			
6:00 p.m.			
7:00 p.m.			
8:00 p.m.			
9:00 p.m.			
10:00 p.m.			
11:00 p.m.			
12:00 a.m.			
1:00 a.m.			

YEAR FOUR FIRST SEMESTER SCHEDULE

THURSDAY	FRIDAY	SATURDAY	SUNDAY

YEAR FOUR SECOND SEMESTER SCHEDULE

	MONDAY	TUESDAY	WEDNESDAY
6:00 a.m.			
7:00 a.m.			
8:00 a.m.			
9:00 a.m.			
10:00 a.m.			
11:00 a.m.			
12:00 p.m.			
1:00 p.m.			
2:00 p.m.			
3:00 p.m.			
4:00 p.m.			
5:00 p.m.			
6:00 p.m.			
7:00 p.m.			
8:00 p.m.			
9:00 p.m.			
10:00 p.m.			
11:00 p.m.			
12:00 a.m.			
1:00 a.m.			

YEAR FOUR SECOND SEMESTER SCHEDULE

THURSDAY	FRIDAY	SATURDAY	SUNDAY

MY COLLEGE MEMORIES

My new living arrangements:

My roommate(s):

Got involved in:

Favorite off campus hang out:

Who I dated:

Favorite tradition:

Best sports moment:

The job I hope to get:

I wish someone would have told me:

_____

_____

_____

_____

_____

_____

_____

_____

Well, now I've revised my goals:

_____

_____

_____

_____

_____

_____

_____

_____

LIFE LESSONS THAT I WILL TAKE WITH ME:

_____

_____

_____

_____

_____

_____

_____

_____

NEW DIRECTION BASED ON WHAT I NOW KNOW:

_____

_____

_____

_____

_____

_____

_____

_____

HOPES FOR MY FUTURE:

_____

_____

_____

_____

_____

_____

_____

_____

THESE ARE THE PEOPLE I
WILL THANK FOREVER:

_____

_____

_____

_____

_____

_____

_____

_____

_____

A NOTE TO MYSELF AS I GRADUATE:

_____
_____
_____
_____
_____
_____
_____
_____
_____
_____
_____
_____
_____
_____
_____
_____
_____
_____
_____
_____
_____

ADVICE I WOULD GIVE TO NEW COLLEGE FRESHMEN:

_____

_____

_____

_____

_____

_____

_____

_____

_____

_____

_____

_____

_____

_____

_____

_____

_____

_____

_____

_____

_____

_____

_____

_____

_____

_____

_____

_____

_____

_____

_____

_____

_____

_____

_____

_____

_____

_____

_____

_____

_____

_____

Thank you for taking the time to peruse this book.
I hope you enjoyed it and that some points resonated
and may make a difference in this amazing journey ahead.
I wish you many wonderful moments as you travel on
the path through college and beyond.

Cindy

ABOUT THE AUTHOR

C indy Laubenstein is an Independent Educational Consultant working out of the North Atlanta area. Cindy founded Aspire College and Career Consulting in 2012 after working in corporate sales and marketing with companies along the East Coast for over 15 years. An Atlanta native, she returned to the area in 2005 and served in various volunteer roles where she developed a college center in a local school that served to educate students and parents on specific colleges, programs of study and the admissions path. After working with a local firm and attending multiple college admissions association educational programs, Cindy decided to launch her own company.

Cindy holds a Bachelor's Degree in Psychology, an MBA, and a Master's in Counseling Studies. She is a member of the:

IECA (Independent Educational Consultants Association),
NACAC (National Association of College Admissions Counselors),
SACAC (Southern Association of College Admissions Counselors)
and HECA (Higher Educational Consultants Association).

To learn more about all services offered, please visit:
http://www.aspirecollegeconsulting.com